WHATEVER STASIS

Cover design & illustration: Shanna Compton
Page design: Tony Mancus

Cover text set in Freight Sans Pro.
Interior text set in Seravek.

Published in the United States of America

ISBN 13: 978-0-9889945-6-0

First Edition

Published by Barrelhouse Books
Baltimore, MD

www.barrelhousemag.com

WHATEVER STASIS

Chris Tonelli

BARRELHOUSE BOOKS

CONTENTS

Economic law inevitably governs our acts and our thoughts.
—Le Corbusier

ELEMENT

        Nothing's not
an archetype;
what we see evolves
as we evolve.

        The will,
in its genetic function,
               scans
for the inevitable
element.

        This
is a technique
           of finance—
the image
and our

       ecstatic newness.

SUBJECT

                    A subject
is an interruption.

Incremental.

They are units
                  of measurement.

                  You pursue
a shapelessness,
accomplish
              a place in time.

(THING)

There deserves
to be nothing.
Who cares
what else.

The arbitrary
thing.

Either way,
it's gone. Or it
stays.

The memory I'd need
to change.

A motif
is too much.

BACKDROP

At the point of indifference,
we abstract our habits;
                          it's the
only way
to be patriotic.

                  It's a better fear,
geometry,
than time—something little
              exerting itself

against the backdrop of something
much larger.

                  An exchange occurs.
                  And vice versa.

OBJECT

                          Everything that ends
has already ended.

Around them
it is quiet. And blank.
            And each
is an object in the blankness.

They call attention to themselves
as a mark upon something.

                              Rituals
that feel like improvisations,
lacking
            something to lack.

(GOD)

                    A poet
is the opposite
of god.

I act out a nostalgia
that becomes
                    my life; we drift
                    further apart.

                    This is
what a symbol is.

FIELD

We can't remember
what was supposed to have changed,
because what we're doing's
                              the same.

We were at the beginning.
We were totally relaxed,
brave,
          thinking all the right things...

               We were rising naïvely
above a field
of countless experiments.

We never made it back to the present.

OBJECT

                There is
one object; there are
no distances.

          You
          are everywhere,
a proper noun.

With what
will you build
this aversion
          to materials?

          And how will you leave?

NIGHT

           Insignificance
makes time travel
possible.

       The arc
of a night,
how a night
         plays out,
         the only
plot.

       The improvved
god.

It's a kind of
         speed
        I'm on.

       If there's something
I should be running from,
I'm not.

       The moon
is our cop;
I'm
   a little revved up.

ACCIDENTS

          Nothing
isn't natural.

Even accidents
are made exclusively
             of matter.

             Leopard
print.
Astro
             turf.

The perfect
uniform.
        The fatal
flaw.

ALTAR

Doves wander
the nature of the yard;
                        it is an
                        altar.

                        When something goes wrong,
                        there is no

death toll.

AREA

                    We
exist in space.

I
                    am not even high right now.

                    If there
is a soul,

it matters
where you are.

A holocaust
of area.
          An intimate holocaust
          repeated.

LOCATION

Objects keep
emptying;
I market
myself to them.

This is my
current location
I say.
It is my
purest expression
to date.

Palette
of debt,
vertical
grief,

I can't
afford all these words.

I can't
get out of here
in time.

I could
succumb
to anything.

EVERYTHING

        Everything's
defined
by everything
it's not.

              By
what's kept out.

You
    are my password;

    avant garde
    is a military term.

SOUVENIR

        Prior to any object,
we've been
somewhere;
            from the center
            of the memory
comes a souvenir.

When we
reapproach an event,
            this
            is the limit
            we are given.

            Like stars,
            like futures,
new pasts are born.
They spread out
            in both directions.

(PLUTO)

          If everything is wrong
eventually,
then everything
           is wrong now.

          I was the planet
Pluto
in a play once;

          I will make the best
ex-husband.

FLAWS

It's difficult
not to do
what we're capable of.

It's difficult to
remember that.

It's difficult
to be wary of
improvements,

examples,

narratives,

images,

memories.

Nothing lasts.

Adjustments are necessary.

Usually removals.

It's difficult,
the realization
that it won't be our
tragic flaws that get us.

Because it will.

(GONE)

                        Trivia.
Year-end
'best of' lists.

                        I can't
even remember
who's dead.

Sometimes,
            a reminder of
            what's not gone
            is a kind of loss,

            what's
still here.

Greed
            is peak
            nihilism.

            How happy
can one be?

(SOMETHING)

There's no such thing
                              as anything,
                              only
what we decide
to capitulate to.

But keep
                              uttering;
                              something
is working from home
in you.

RECEPTION

            Dreams,
my reception
is bad.

Beautiful and worthy subjects
are everywhere,
                which is
                out of reach.

Things begin
and end.
        In between,
        there is an order—a slow
                            avalanche
of all
I fail
            to appreciate.

            Dreams?
            Come in.

            Don't leave me
to a whole day
filled
        with what I
        have to decide.

I'd have
no idea
            what to record.
            What
to report.

JOKE

On the interstate,
a smear of nature.
A recycled
portrait.

A practical
joke.

I listen to
sports radio, eat
routine bars.

EVIDENCE

I don't
        get
        the survival instinct.

       In
finite things, in
infinite things.

Being spoiled
is evidence
        of over-evolution.

          The death
wish.
The grief
         economy.

         Strategic
animals,
imaginative
       animals,

       there aren't
       very many thoughts.

       There's an abyss
you've lost,
but it's not the only
          abyss there is.

VERSION

          There is
no god.

Only
          that feeling.

          Only some
          other bad

version of yourself.

THEM

        The unknown
is sacred;
don't insult it

                        by guessing.

                        If you can't
hear them breathing,
you don't
        know they're breathing.

(SAFETY)

    The capacity
for two lives.
The inability
    to choose.

    When a myth
    induces faith,
death—life's safety—
is removed.

   A wild gift
in a
tidy package.

    The boner spam
I get at work.

ORNAMENT

Every ornament
is a decoy
       we set for ourselves.

          Our
primitive gratitude
must leave us—this
is where it goes.

       I express
       the feeling
I would give
a real deer;
       birds gather
       at the feeder.

When I think of no hope,
I get no
      sadder.

TECHNOLOGIES

I have a long history
of underreacting.
                Of
                overreacting.

                My
                sacred identities.

                    I make
Kendrick Lamar memes
with pictures of my daughter
wearing water wings.

                    I have trouble
discerning which technologies
will last long enough
to feature
                in my poesie.

              But I have
no problem
purchasing them.

CRIMES

                Everything's
a stunt.

A gimmick.

                That's the
                one shared identity,
the one
human way to act.

                      Human nature?
                      Maybe only
certain crimes.

Maybe only
        every
        exertion,
every
confrontation.

                The word
                deserve.

                Tenure.

CLOTHES

          Sometimes,
it's as dull
as it should be.

I iron
little clothes.

          We're not
here for very long.

FUNCTION

                    Action
is often a solution
to an anxiety—a technology
                    of curation

                    casting hope
                    to where the memory
waits.

A thing desiring
to document
                              a function.

                              Sounds
that sound like sense;
parts
        per million.

WHAT

A craving
                        is a kind of
                        propaganda.

                        We
do not repeat mistakes;
they
        are a language
        that survives in us.

                                It's hard to say
how close to death you've come
while feeling confident.

It's hard to know
what not to
                fend off.

SUNS

                  Hurtling
toward something inevitable,
I'm addicted
        to stopping.

       Time
is a kind of
persecution, a kind
of forgiveness.

        Eventually,
        even what happens
        never happened,

        a universe
        of suns.

        I wonder
        if we'll
ever be ready
for a
    new reward.

(BELIEF)

There's an energy
that remains dormant
when there's no longer
an object of belief.

An effort.

A herd.

Sometimes, I
exercise.

(ARCHETYPE)

         You imagine yourself
one archetype.
But probably not one
               who does so;
               each moment,
two myths.

         Your job
         is to prevent this.

DELTA

Deciding.

The false sense
of exerting
the will.

Then,
a discrepancy.

The delta.

This
strangest other
we're in.

WHAT

                        A body
is a forgetting machine,
regenerates with
                    what hasn't left—a net
                    increase
in uselessness
on the way
            to equilibrium.

            Post-consequence,
            post-
extinction
entropy (ß).

Functional poverty,
magic relies
            on any number
            of ignorances—I am in
                            none
of my favorite categories.

            A truth
always leads
to its
        logical conclusion.

        And so does
        what's false.

                    I've never
been able
to distinguish between things.

I've always
           given myself
           the -ish.

TRACE

First, there must be
                    a presence.

                    Something
                    very simple.

                    A trace of existence
hinted at.

An object
in the field of vision.

                        A distance
                        marked.

To activate the mind,
suggest only
                    the very least
                    by which a thing
                    can be defined.

                    And then
remove it.

ACT

In the lawn,
          a deletion.
          Then,
time.

          An act
forgotten by
the space the act created.

    Something
    grows over, fills
in.

The wrong act.

The wrong space, where
the substance resumes.

(ANYTHING)

What's displaced
when something suddenly
exists?

The feeling of knowing
and maybe even
knowing?

I eat a radish
with butter and salt.
The sycamores
edit the sun.

It's impossible
to witness anything;
why bother
other things?

DEBRIS

Each moment survives
        by evolving
until it
never happened.

                In its place,
a thing.
It radiates
        a glacier.

        A vacation.

        A religion.

        An entire
dimension to excavate.

                What
to get close enough to
to recover
        what?

        A memory.
A moment's
debris.
        Whatever's removed
        to make room
        for the device.

        For us.

SCALE

　　　　My body
heals—an aesthetic
　　　　　　　　of scale.

　　　　　　　　My body won't
heal in time.

ERA

The teller at the bank
has feathered hair—her better
era.

I am getting
more and more
amateur.

It never
fails—the numb resignation
a cloud gives off.

(SOMETHING)

        Evolution
is a process
by which things
            become extinct.

           My only evidence
           is that I'm a better person
in my daydreams.

In the old days,
            our primal thoughts
            gave way to our
industrious actions.

What would I have drawn
on the walls of my cave?
                 And who
would've eventually found it?

It's impossible
           to be redundant
           without something
           in the first place.

BODY

              A bomb
doesn't arrive;
your body
        opens again.

          What they
remove
determines what
              season begins.

An organ: fall.
          A baby:
fall.

SHAPE

             An object.
             Or maybe just the desire
to be its shape. Its
surface tension.
             The fate
of that shape.
The prison.

         Exempt.

         Invisible.

The balance between
language and sense,
where chance leads
to something tangible.

DATA

It takes
two mistakes—

        you

        and another,
        patient enough to know
        that nothing about you
        is real,

besides the patterns you make
and maybe why.

        Your data,
        their blind spot.

        A vigilant love.

MURDERER

                    I promise
not to drink coffee
after 3 pm
ever again.

                    In the dark,
I am a father.
In the dark,
                I am a murderer
                not murdering.

                    I get up
to check on my son;
the lawn
            has my house
            surrounded.

SURPRISES

                      Now's emotion
constantly arrives,
then burns off.

Reveals
                       whatever stasis.

                      Two
numbing surprises.
What's
      left to regard?

NEED

I.
In order for there to be a recurrence,
there have to be differences
in the elements of a set.

For there to be a pattern,
there has to be a theme.

II.
                Need
may be the only
recurrence—an archetype
so large
        it's hard to recall
        what's been replaced
        to keep meeting it.

III.
               An object
is a unit of place.
If there is only
        one object, it is
        the place.

We don't take comfort
in what's familiar,
             but what recurs.

MISTAKES

When the expression of desire
                        is new,
                        we make the same mistakes
a candidate makes.

We listen to them
over and over.

            It's a
            clever therapy;
            it's a tangible,
objective
fairness.

                The lawn mower
                is a violent
                omnivore;

                my son says
grass for the first time.

ARCHIVE

       The body
is a map,
an archive
of the Stockholm syndrome

                I have for myself,

             grateful

for the limitations
I'm allowed,

the weaknesses
       I repeat.

      It's a
fine line
between self-awareness

        and getting worse.

SURPRISE

               Disappointment
should imply at least
some element
        of surprise.

        The idea of earning.

        A sense of justice.

        A version of fun
        that isn't annoying.

ADULTHOOD

I saw
a band.
They had
a uniform feeling.

Adulthood
is the state of not wanting
what you're jealous of.

SOMETHING

                          Content
is what's important,
not
                   what kind.

                   Starlight.
                   The death
it should imply.

                       Sometimes,
being warned means
it's already happened;

sometimes,
                   I want something
                   to loom.

THINGS

         Decisions
were the
fundamental particles;

                the will,
                a collective celebrity.

                The few
                conceivable things
were all improvements,
and we achieved them.

FACTORY

I.
                Context
is a synthesis
of what has occurred;

                      then,
                      an occurrence factory.

                      We get
used to things.

Definitions.

What counts.

Casualties
            of an evolving
            reverence.

II.
                Mood
is a technology
of temporariness
                  and value;

a lawn
        is a field
where a field once was.

WHATEVER

                    I believe
in the order
in which things come.

The only way
                    to destroy them
                    is to bring them here.

                    Whatever comes
                    is whatever comes.

Art
        without art.

END

           Progress
has no intentions;
things
           run their course.

          Local evolutions.

          Local extinctions.

          A rising action.

          All the wrong nows.

          It will feel
like the end.
It will feel like this
          until the end.

ACKNOWLEDGEMENTS

Thank you to the editors of *Big Lucks*, *Coldfront*, *DIG*, *Fou*, *Gigantic Sequins*, *Gulf Coast*, *jubilat*, *La Fovea*, *Lute & Drum*, *Leveler*, *Pretty LIT*, *Sixth Finch*, *Tenderloin*, and *Fuck Poems: An Exceptional Anthology* for publishing versions of some of these poems. Special thanks to Jeremiah Gould of Rye House Press for including versions of some of these poems in the chapbook *Increment*.

ABOUT THE AUTHOR

Chris Tonelli is a founding editor of the independent poetry press, Birds, LLC, and he curates the So & So Series and edits *So & So Magazine*. He is the author of five chapbooks and one other full-length collection, *The Trees Around* (Birds, LLC). He works in the Libraries at NC State and co-owns So & So Books in downtown Raleigh, where he lives with his wife, Allison, and their two kids, Miles and Vera.